AN OLD FASHIONED KEEPBOOK™

A Birthday Book

DATES TO REMEMBER FOREVER

Edited by Linda Campbell Franklin
Designed by Sara Bowman

Tree Communications, Inc.
New York

Cover fabric design © 1980 Cranston Print
Works Company

Published in the United States by
Tree Communications, Inc.,
250 Park Avenue South, New York,
New York 10003.
Printed in the United States of America.
ISBN 0-934504-06-7

This book was typeset in Janson by
David E. Seham Associates, Inc. Color
separations were made by National
Colorgraphics, Inc. The paper is 70 lb.
Warren Olde Style, cream, supplied by
Baldwin Paper Company. The book was
printed and bound by R. R. Donnelley &
Sons Company.

I very much appreciate the thoughtful help
given by Ruth Forst Michel and Pamela
Green in shaping this book. And to
Cyanocitta cristata, gracias, mi amigo.

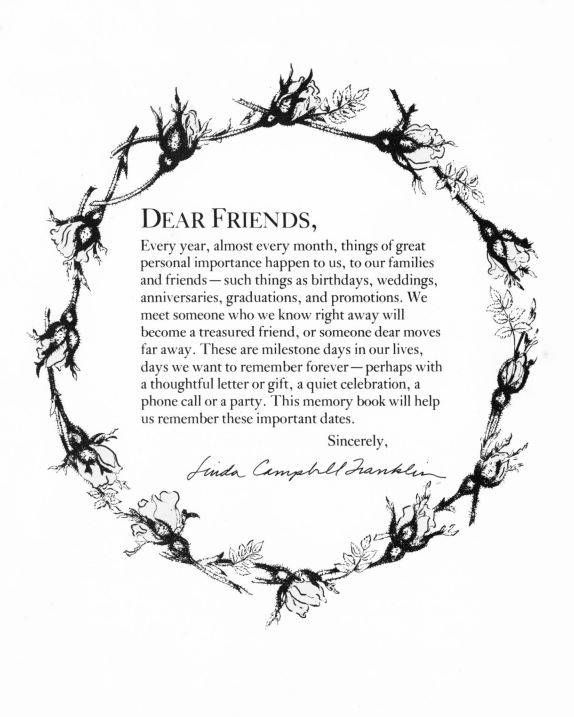

Dear Friends,

Every year, almost every month, things of great personal importance happen to us, to our families and friends — such things as birthdays, weddings, anniversaries, graduations, and promotions. We meet someone who we know right away will become a treasured friend, or someone dear moves far away. These are milestone days in our lives, days we want to remember forever — perhaps with a thoughtful letter or gift, a quiet celebration, a phone call or a party. This memory book will help us remember these important dates.

Sincerely,

Linda Campbell Franklin

Forecasting the Future
with Nursery Rhymes

Born on Monday, fair in the face.
Born on Tuesday, full of God's grace.
Born on Wednesday, best to be had.
Born on Thursday, merry and glad.
Born on Friday, worthily given.
Born on Saturday, work hard for a living.
Born on Sunday, shall never know want.

Monday's bairn is fair of face,
Tuesday's bairn is full of grace,
Wednesday's bairn is full of woe,
Thursday's bairn has far to go,
Friday's bairn is loving and giving,
Saturday's bairn works hard for its living,
But the bairn that is born on the Sabbath day
Is bonny and blithe, and good and gay.

JANUARY

January brings the snow,
Makes our feet and fingers glow.

BIRTHSTONE: GARNET

FLOWERS OF THE MONTH: CARNATION, SNOWDROP

NAME	OCCASION	YEAR

JANUARY 1

JANUARY 2

JANUARY 3

THE VINE

The wine of Love is music,
    And the feast of Love is song:
When Love sits down to banquet,
    Love sits long:

Sits long and rises drunken,
    But not with the feast and the wine,
He reeleth with his own heart,
    That great, rich Vine.

        James Thomson

NAME	OCCASION	YEAR

JANUARY 4

JANUARY 5

JANUARY 6

JANUARY 7

here is not always a 'thaw' in January, nor do all spring-like days in winter come in January. As the old-fashioned almanacs would put it, scattering the words down the page for January: *About — this — time — expect — several — warm — days.* Even if the 'about this time' were the last of February, the country people would regard it as 'our January thaw, only about a month late this year!' The first of these warm days is often cloudy, and so misty and cloudy that the ground seems to steam. The snow that may have fallen two or three weeks ago is nearly all melted. Then how slushy it is!— how 'disagreeable getting about,' the older folks would say."

From *St. Nicholas* magazine, January 1904

NAME	OCCASION	YEAR

JANUARY 8

JANUARY 9

JANUARY 10

"The most useless day of all is that in which we have not laughed."

Sebastien R. N. Chamfort

NAME	OCCASION	YEAR

JANUARY 11

JANUARY 12

JANUARY 13

JANUARY 14

AROMATIC VINEGARS

Throughout this book will appear nineteenth century recipes for making aromatic vinegars — described in the words of the editor of *Scammell's Treasure-House of Knowledge* [1891] as "aromatics . . . highly esteemed as reviving perfumes, both for the toilette and the sick room. They are generally dropped on a small piece of sponge placed in a stoppered bottle or vinaigrette." While we do not call for the return of swooning, perhaps the fragrances will be welcome in their own right!

The directions usually say "macerate." This term means to infuse without heat. The aromatic substances are soaked for a matter of weeks in room temperature liquid. The liquid thereby absorbs the perfume. The resulting vinegar infusion is *not* used on salads.

NAME	OCCASION	YEAR
JANUARY 15		
JANUARY 16		
JANUARY 17		

LAVENDER VINEGAR

One pound of fresh lavender flowers; 12 pounds of best vinegar. Macerate.

NAME	OCCASION	YEAR

JANUARY 18

JANUARY 19

JANUARY 20

JANUARY 21

On land and sea,
    when water's deep,
And man a crisis faces,
A good plan is to try to keep
His mouth shut in both cases.

NAME	OCCASION	YEAR

JANUARY 22

JANUARY 23

JANUARY 24

"In skating over thin ice our safety is our speed."

Ralph Waldo Emerson

NAME	OCCASION	YEAR

JANUARY 25

JANUARY 26

JANUARY 27

"Heaven knows
we need never be
ashamed of
our tears, for
they are rain
upon the blinding
dust of earth,
overlying our
hard hearts."

JANUARY 28

From *Great Expectations* by
Charles Dickens

PRESERVING WITH GLYCERIN

Autumn foliage, small branches of fruit trees, eucalyptus, evergreen boughs, holly branches, and many other woody-stemmed plants can be preserved with glycerin, which is available at almost any drugstore.

Split one to two inches of the branch end; put the cut branch in a solution of two parts water, one part glycerin, in a jar or vase. Leave the branch in the solution for up to three weeks, or until you see beads of glycerin on the leaf tips. Hang the boughs upside down to dry for about two weeks before using. The leaves will remain flexible and will not fall off.

NAME	OCCASION	YEAR

JANUARY 29

JANUARY 30

JANUARY 31

FEBRUARY

February brings the rain,
Thaws the frozen lake again.

BIRTHSTONE: AMETHYST   FLOWERS OF THE MONTH: PRIMROSE, VIOLET

NAME	OCCASION	YEAR

FEBRUARY 1

FEBRUARY 2

The rose will cease to blow,
  The eagle turn a dove,
The stream will cease to flow,
  Ere I will cease to love.

The sun will cease to shine,
  The world will cease to move,
The stars their light resign,
  Ere I will cease to love.

From a mid-nineteenth century
Valentine

FEBRUARY 3

Sorrow and the scarlet leaf,
    Sad thoughts and sunny weather:
Ah me, this glory and this grief
    Agree not well together!

From *A Song for September* by Thomas William Parsons

NAME	OCCASION	YEAR

FEBRUARY 4

FEBRUARY 5

FEBRUARY 6

FEBRUARY 7

If music be the food of love, play on;
Give me excess of it, that, surfeiting,
The appetite may sicken, and so die.
That strain again! It had a dying fall:
O! it came o'er my ear like the sweet sound
That breathes upon a bank of violets,
Stealing and giving odour!"

From *Twelfth-Night* by William Shakespeare

NAME	OCCASION	YEAR

FEBRUARY 8

FEBRUARY 9

FEBRUARY 10

NAME	OCCASION	YEAR

FEBRUARY 11

FEBRUARY 12

FEBRUARY 13

FEBRUARY 14

CANADA LILY

Blue! Gentle cousin of the forest-green,
Married to green in all the sweetest flowers,—
Forget-me-not,—the blue bell,—and, that Queen
Of secrecy, the violet.

From *Sonnet, Blue* by John Keats

NAME	OCCASION	YEAR

FEBRUARY 15

FEBRUARY 16

FEBRUARY 17

NAME	OCCASION	YEAR

FEBRUARY 18

FEBRUARY 19

FEBRUARY 20

FEBRUARY 21

A violet by a mossy stone
Half hidden from the eye! —
Fair as a star, when only one
Is shining in the sky.

From *Lucy: She Dwelt Among the Untrodden Ways*
by William Wordsworth

The he violet loves a sunny bank,
The cowslip loves the lea;
The scarlet creeper loves the elm,
But I love—thee.

From *Proposal* by Bayard Taylor

NAME	OCCASION	YEAR

FEBRUARY 22

_____

_____

_____

_____

_____

FEBRUARY 23

_____

_____

_____

_____

FEBRUARY 24

_____

_____

_____

_____

NAME	OCCASION	YEAR

FEBRUARY 25

FEBRUARY 26

RECIPE FOR COFFEE

Black as the devil,
Hot as hell,
Pure as an angel,
Sweet as love.

       Talleyrand

FEBRUARY 27

FEBRUARY 28

NAME	OCCASION	YEAR

FEBRUARY 29

_____

_____

_____

_____

_____

_____

_____

Look Before You Leap!

Leap Year on Monday — well-doing the men are.
Leap Year on Tuesday — handsome the men are.
Leap Year on Wednesday — true-hearted the men are.
Leap Year on Thursday — hard-working the men are.
Leap Year on Friday — careful the men are.
Leap Year on Saturday — obliging the men are.
Leap Year on Sunday — _all_ men are good.

Eight-hundred years ago a Scottish law gave "mayden ladyes of both high and lowe estait" liberty to ask for a man's hand in marriage on Leap Year Day. We just missed the 1980 Leap Year, which fell on a Friday.

MARCH

March brings breezes, loud and shrill,
To stir the dancing daffodil.

Grandville del

Ch. Geoffroy sc

BIRTHSTONES: AQUAMARINE, BLOODSTONE   FLOWERS OF THE MONTH: JONQUIL, DAFFODIL

Learn the sweet magic
of a cheerful face;
Not always smiling,
but at least serene.

From *The Morning Visit*
by Oliver Wendell Holmes

NAME	OCCASION	YEAR

MARCH 1

MARCH 2

MARCH 3

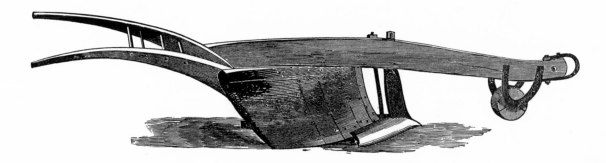

NAME	OCCASION	YEAR

MARCH 4

MARCH 5

One to rot, and one to grow,
One for the pigeon
        and one for the crow.

*That's the folk rule for planting beans:
plant four if you want one to grow in
your garden.*

MARCH 6

MARCH 7

Sweet, sweet is the greeting of eyes,
And sweet is the voice in its greeting,
When adieus have grown old and goodbyes
Fade away where old Time is retreating.

Warm the nerve of a welcoming hand,
And earnest a kiss on the brow,
When we meet over sea and o'er land
Where furrows are new to the plough.

John Keats

NAME	OCCASION	YEAR
MARCH 8		
MARCH 9		
MARCH 10		

"There's no sauce in the world like hunger."

Miguel de Cervantes

NAME	OCCASION	YEAR

MARCH 11

MARCH 12

MARCH 13

MARCH 14

"The finer the sense for the beautiful and the lovely, and the fairer and lovelier the object presented to the sense; the more exquisite the individual's capacity of joy, and the more ample his means and opportunities of enjoyment, the more heavily will he feel the ache of solitariness, the more unsubstantial becomes the feast spread around him."

From *The Blossoming of the Solitary Date-Tree* by Samuel Taylor Coleridge

Maple Sugar Camp

 mong the few festivities peculiar to New England, none is more agreeable, or suggests a more real healthful amusement than maple sugar making. In Western Massachusetts, Vermont, and New Hampshire, the 'sugar orchard' yields what is quite a source of wealth; in fact, in the annual statistics the 'crop' figures up quite a number of thousand pounds, and large communities use very little else, to sweeten their social existence, so far as it depends upon coffee and tea, to say nothing of hot buckwheat cakes. The sugar boiling generally takes place in some romantic spot—in some quiet valley, or pleasant hill side.

NAME	OCCASION	YEAR
MARCH 15		
MARCH 16		
MARCH 17		

NAME	OCCASION	YEAR

MARCH 18

MARCH 19

MARCH 20

MARCH 21

The streams, just released from their winter captivity, along with the trout dance merrily in the newly recovered freedom, the groves fill up with feathered songsters—the sap runs merrily from the bark girdled trees, the maple molasses is delicious, and in its crystalyzed form it is perfection itself.

"One thing is curious about maple sugar gatherings. All the little unfinished love affairs of the year are brought at these trysting places to a joyful termination. It is no matter how hard has been the heart of Aramintha, or Clotile through the winter months, just let them breathe the invigorating airs of spring, taste maple sugar, and they yield to the prayers of the expectant strains, and the two, melt into one as lovingly, as two small pieces of sugar, by virtue of a birch bark fire, become melted into one inseparable and never to be perfectly divided cake."

Picture and text from *Frank Leslie's Illustrated Newspaper*, March 29, 1856.

an was not born merely to eat, drink, sleep, or to spend his time in hunting, shooting, gaming, idleness, dissipation, and sensual gratifications; but to be industrious and useful to society; and ought to leave some records of his actions as a testimonial of his endeavours, at least, to be useful to the present and future generations.

"Men pursue different objects as their inclinations and fancies lead them; but of all the arts, agriculture, when properly conducted, is one of the most useful, profitable, pleasing, rational and healthful amusements in life."

From *The Pennsylvania Farmer*
by Job Roberts, 1804

NAME	OCCASION	YEAR
MARCH 22		
MARCH 23		
MARCH 24		

"In Nature there is nothing melancholy."

Samuel Taylor Coleridge

NAME	OCCASION	YEAR

MARCH 25

MARCH 26

MARCH 27

MARCH 28

THE REASON

Says John last night:
    "William, by grab! I'm beat
To know why stolen kisses
    Taste so sweet."

Says William: "Sho!
    That's easily explained—
It's 'cause they're *syrup-*
    titiously obtained."

Ironquill

SUNSET

Now the sun is sinking
    In the golden west;
Birds and bees and children
    All have gone to rest;
And the merry streamlet,
    As it runs along,
With a voice of sweetness
    Sings its evening song.

Cowslip, daisy, violet,
    In their little beds,
All among the grasses
    Hide their heavy heads;
There they'll all,
        sweet darlings,
    Lie in the happy dreams,
Till the rosy morning
    Wakes them with its beams.

From *McGuffey's Third Reader*

NAME	OCCASION	YEAR
MARCH 29		
MARCH 30		
MARCH 31		

APRIL

April weather:
Rain and sunshine, both together.

BIRTHSTONE: DIAMOND

FLOWERS OF THE MONTH: DAISY, SWEET PEA

ANSWER TO A CHILD'S QUESTION

Do you ask what the birds say? The Sparrow, the Dove,/ The Linnet and Thrush say, "I love and I love!"/ In the winter they're silent—the wind is so strong,/ What it says, I don't know, but it sings a loud song./ But green leaves, and blossoms, and sunny warm weather,/ And singing, and loving—all come back together,/ But the lark is so brimful of gladness and love,/ The green fields below him, the blue sky above,/ That he sings, and he sings: and for ever sings he—/ "I love my Love, and my Love loves me!"

Samuel Taylor Coleridge

NAME	OCCASION	YEAR
APRIL 1		
APRIL 2		
APRIL 3		

NAME	OCCASION	YEAR

APRIL 4

APRIL 5

APRIL 6

APRIL 7

MONKEYING AROUND WITH
THE ROSES

Banana skins, being rich in
sulphur, phosphates,
magnesium, calcium and other
fertilizing elements, are great
for rose gardens. Put them just
below the surface, near the
rose bush. This should work
especially well with climbing
roses!

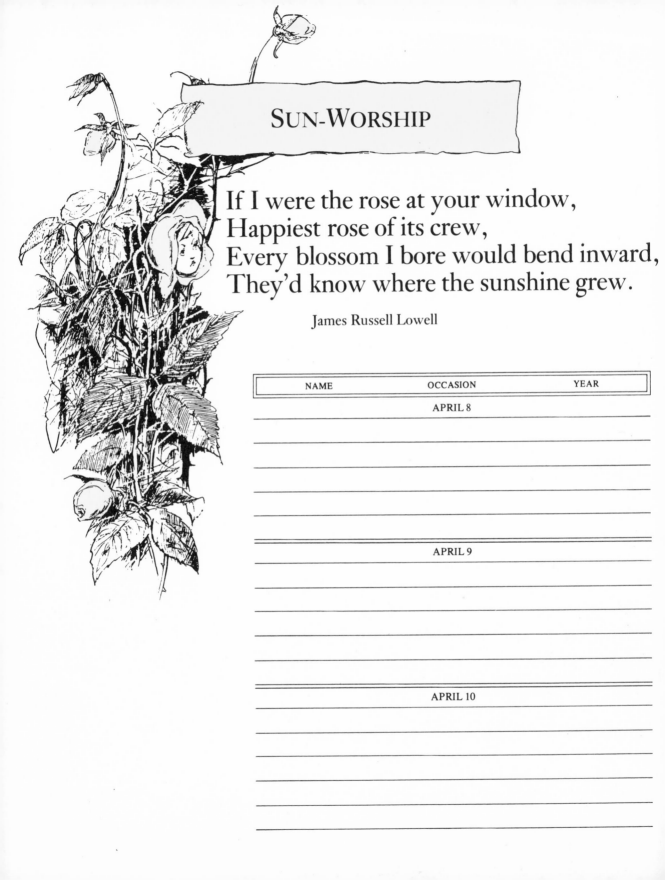

SUN-WORSHIP

If I were the rose at your window,
Happiest rose of its crew,
Every blossom I bore would bend inward,
They'd know where the sunshine grew.

James Russell Lowell

NAME	OCCASION	YEAR
APRIL 8		
APRIL 9		
APRIL 10		

RIDDLE

In what place did the cock crow when all the world could hear him?*

NAME	OCCASION	YEAR

APRIL 11

APRIL 12

APRIL 13

APRIL 14

* *In Noab's Ark.*

mall
service is true
service while it
lasts./ Of
humblest friends,
bright creature!
scorn not one:/
The daisy, by the
shadow that it
casts,/ Protects
the lingering
dewdrop from
the sun.

From *To a Child, Written in Her Album* by William Wordsworth

NAME	OCCASION	YEAR

APRIL 15

APRIL 16

APRIL 17

"If we walk in the woods, we must feed mosquitoes."

Ralph Waldo Emerson

NAME	OCCASION	YEAR

APRIL 18

APRIL 19

APRIL 20

APRIL 21

April

When April,
one day, was asked
whether
She *could* make reliable
weather,
She laughed till she cried,
And said "Bless you I've tried,
But the things will get
mixed up together."

NAME	OCCASION	YEAR

APRIL 22

APRIL 23

APRIL 24

"For, lo! the winter is past, the rain is over and gone; the flowers appear on the earth; the time of the singing of birds is come, and the voice of the turtle is heard in our land."

From *The Song of Solomon*, *The Bible, Old Testament*

The poet pointed where a flower,
A simple daisy, starred the sod,
. . . "Proof of love and power
Behold, behold a smile of God!"

From *A Thought* by William Cox Bennett

NAME	OCCASION	YEAR

APRIL 25

APRIL 26

APRIL 27

APRIL 28

"Every fruit or berry has its mission to man hidden away within it. Therefore, set out a strawberry bed, if you haven't got one . . . Plant currants. . . . Border the fence with raspberries. Walk around your place during the early spring days, and make a mental inventory of every spot where you can stick in a fruit tree or a berry bush. Plant something."

From a nineteenth-century health guide, as quoted in *The Great Patent Medicine Era* by Adelaide Hechtlinger

NAME	OCCASION	YEAR

APRIL 29

APRIL 30

MAY

May brings flocks of pretty lambs,
Skipping by their fleecy dams.

BIRTHSTONE: EMERALD   FLOWERS OF THE MONTH: HAWTHORNE, LILY-OF-THE-VALLEY

It is said that if humans want to see the faeries, all they have to do is put a four-leaf clover in a hat, and wear it.

NAME	OCCASION	YEAR

MAY 1

MAY 2

MAY 3

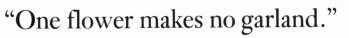

"One flower makes no garland."

George Herbert

NAME	OCCASION	YEAR

MAY 4

Who thought of the lilac?
"I," dew said,
"I made up the lilac
out of my head."

From *The Lilac*
by Humbert Wolfe

MAY 5

MAY 6

MAY 7

Growing a Thorn Hedge

"In growing haws, to have a
good live fence, there must not
only be ditches with the
hedges, but also a close
attention is to be observed to
weed and keep the soil clean,
and the hedge defended from
cattle and sheep, especially
during the first three or four
years; and the young plants are
to be often visited, and may or
not be trained to grow
entwined together; but the
branches are to be shortened
from time to time, and in due
time the whole may be
plashed*.

"Gaps on these visits are to
be looked for, and stopped
before they become frequented
by hogs, dogs or boys."

From *The Pennsylvania Farmer*
by Job Roberts, 1804
Plashed means braided or entwined.

NAME	OCCASION	YEAR
	MAY 8	
	MAY 9	
	MAY 10	

"A hedge between keeps friendship green."

An old *Mother Goose* saying

NAME	OCCASION	YEAR

MAY 11

MAY 12

MAY 13

MAY 14

"As the well-trimmed lawn and the cleanly kept park, with no unsightly weeds or piles of rubbish to meet the gaze, are objects of admiration, so the neatly-kept page of writing, marred by no blots or stains, is beautiful to the eye."

From *Hill's Manual of Social and Business Forms* by Thomas E. Hill, 1905

ou must not know too much, or be too precise or scientific about birds and trees and flowers and water-craft; a certain free margin, and even vagueness—perhaps ignorance, credulity—helps your enjoyment of these things."

From *Specimen Days. Birds. May 14, 1881* by Walt Whitman

NAME	OCCASION	YEAR

MAY 15

MAY 16

MAY 17

I find earth not gray but rosy,
  Heaven not grim but fair of hue.
Do I stoop? I pluck a posy.
  Do I stand and stare? All's blue.

From *At the "Mermaid"* by Robert Browning

NAME	OCCASION	YEAR

MAY 18

MAY 19

MAY 20

MAY 21

 A May Song

The orchard is a rosy cloud,
   The oak a rosy mist,
And oh, the gold of the buttercups
   The morning sun has kissed!
There are twinkling shadows on the grass
   Of a myriad tiny leaves,
And a twittering loud from the busy crowd
   That build beneath the eaves.
      Then sing, happy children,
        The bird and bee are here,
     The May time is a gay time,
       The blossom time o' the year.

A message comes across the fields,
   Borne on the balmy air,
For all the little seeking hands
   There are flowers enough and to spare.
Hark! a murmuring in the hive, —
   List! a carol clear and sweet, —
While feathered throats the thrilling notes
   A thousand times repeat.
      Then sing, happy children,
        The bird and bee are here,
     The May time is a gay time,
       The blossom time o' the year.

By Anna M. Pratt, *St. Nicholas* magazine, May 1889

NAME	OCCASION	YEAR
MAY 22		
MAY 23		
MAY 24		

NAME	OCCASION	YEAR

MAY 25

MAY 26

MAY 27

MAY 28

he lily is an herb with a white flower. And though the leaves of the flower be white yet within shineth the likeness of gold."

Bartholomaeus Anglicus, thirteenth century

NAME	OCCASION	YEAR
MAY 29		
MAY 30		
MAY 31		

JUNE

June brings tulips, lilies, roses,
Fills the children's hands with posies.

BIRTHSTONES: MOONSTONE, ALEXANDRITE, PEARL

FLOWERS OF THE MONTH:
ROSE, HONEYSUCKLE

To Make Rose Beads

In order to make a whole necklace of rose beads you will need between 30 and 45 roses. Pick them in the late morning when they are dry, and remove the stems. Chop the flowers into fine pieces and place in a saucepan. Add water to barely cover, and simmer gently for about an hour. Add small amounts of water when necessary. Allow the mixture to cool, then simmer again for at least a half-hour. Strain the pulp and shape into beads with your fingers. Use a heavy-gauge upholstery needle to make the holes. Dry the beads on a piece of paper; it may take a day or longer. String the rose beads and wear them around your neck: they will give off the scent of roses.

NAME	OCCASION	YEAR
	JUNE 1	
	JUNE 2	
	JUNE 3	

NAME	OCCASION	YEAR

JUNE 4

JUNE 5

JUNE 6

Though the rose scent dies and the rose decays / The rose of the spirit never is sere; / Soft as roses be all thy ways, / And thou, may'st thou through all thy days, / Open and greaten, even as these, / Petal by petal and year by year.

JUNE 7

Oh, my luve is like a red, red rose,
    That's newly sprung in June;
Oh, my luve is like the melodie,
    That's sweetly played in tune.

From *A Red, Red Rose* by Robert Burns

NAME	OCCASION	YEAR
JUNE 8		
JUNE 9		
JUNE 10		

NAME	OCCASION	YEAR

JUNE 11

_____
_____
_____
_____
_____
_____

JUNE 12

_____
_____
_____
_____
_____
_____

JUNE 13

_____
_____
_____
_____
_____
_____

JUNE 14

_____
_____
_____
_____
_____
_____

How doth the little busy bee
   Improve each shining hour,
And gather honey all the day
   From every opening flower!

From _Divine Songs_
by Isaac Watts

nd what is so rare as a day in June?
Then, if ever, come perfect days;
Then Heaven tries the earth if it be in tune,
And over it softly her warm ear lays.

From *The Vision of Sir Launfal* by James Russell Lowell

NAME	OCCASION	YEAR
JUNE 15		
JUNE 16		
JUNE 17		

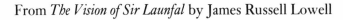

The First Rose of Summer

"Oh, dear! is summer over?"
    I heard a rosebud moan,
When first her eyes she opened,
    And found she was alone.

"Oh, why did summer leave me,
    Little me, belated?
Where are the other roses?
    I think they *might* have waited!"

NAME	OCCASION	YEAR

JUNE 18

JUNE 19

JUNE 20

JUNE 21

Soon the little rosebud
    Saw to her surprise
Other roses opening,
    So she dried her eyes.

Then I heard her laughing
    Gayly in the sun,
"I thought the summer over;
    Why it's only just begun!"

By O. Herford, *St. Nicholas* magazine,
June 1889

Where are the dear, old-fashioned posies,
Quaint in form and bright in hue,
Such as grandma gave her lovers
When she walked the garden through?

From *Old-Fashioned Flowers* by Ethel Lynn Beers

NAME	OCCASION	YEAR
JUNE 22		
JUNE 23		
JUNE 24		

NAME	OCCASION	YEAR

JUNE 25

_____

_____

_____

_____

_____

_____

JUNE 26

_____

_____

_____

_____

_____

_____

JUNE 27

_____

_____

_____

_____

_____

Baby said
  When she smelt the rose,
"Oh! what a pity
  I've only one nose!"

From *The Difference*
by Laura Elizabeth Richards

JUNE 28

_____

_____

_____

_____

_____

N othing is so like a soul as a bee. It goes from flower to flower as a soul from star to star, and it gathers honey as a soul gathers light."

Victor Hugo

NAME	OCCASION	YEAR

JUNE 29

JUNE 30

JULY

Hot July brings cooling showers,
Apricots, and gillyflowers.

BIRTHSTONE: RUBY   FLOWERS OF THE MONTH: WATER LILY, LARKSPUR, DELPHINIUM

To Extract Odors of Flowers

rocure a quantity of the petals of any flower of an agreeable odor; card* thin layers of cotton wool, which dip into the finest Florence oil**; sprinkle a small quantity of fine salt on the flowers, and place layers of flowers and cotton, alternately, until an earthen or wide-mouthed glass vessel is quite full; tie the top closed, and lay in a south aspect exposed to the sun, and in 15 days a fragrant oil may be squeezed away from the whole mass; little inferior, if roses are used, to the dear and highly valued otto or odor of roses."

From *Scammell's Treasure-House of Knowledge 1891*

NAME	OCCASION	YEAR
JULY 1		
JULY 2		
JULY 3		

*Card means to comb out, disentangle or pull out and stretch fibers.

**Florence oil is a very fine oil used as a perfume base. It is commonly known now as orris or orrisroot oil. Bottles of it are available from some natural or homeopathic pharmacies and herb stores. It comes from the iris root—called the rhizome—and there are not many shady gardens where you cannot grow the iris. To serve as a perfume fixative, the rhizome is pressed to make oil, or is dried and then ground, powdered, or thinly sliced.

NAME	OCCASION	YEAR

JULY 4

JULY 5

JULY 6

JULY 7

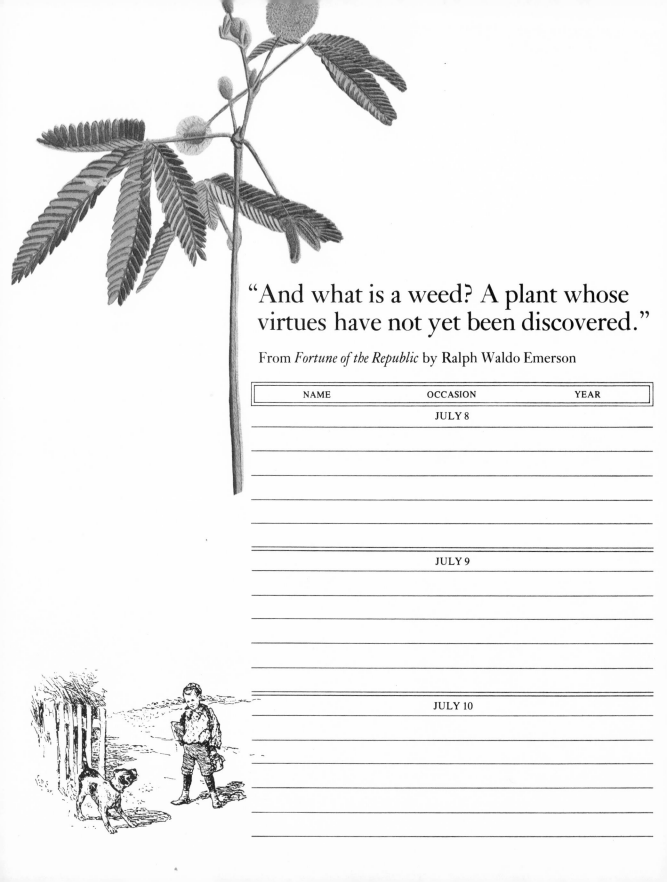

"And what is a weed? A plant whose virtues have not yet been discovered."

From *Fortune of the Republic* by Ralph Waldo Emerson

NAME	OCCASION	YEAR

JULY 8

JULY 9

JULY 10

"A weed is no more than a flower in disguise."

From *A Fable for Critics* by James Russell Lowell

NAME	OCCASION	YEAR

JULY 11

JULY 12

JULY 13

JULY 14

"The walker makes the acquaintance of all the weeds. They are travelers like himself, the tramps of the vegetable world. They are going east, west, north, south; they walk, they fly, they swim, they steal a ride, they travel by rail, by flood, by wind; they go underground, and they go above, across lots and by the highway, But, like other tramps, they find it safest by the highway; in the fields they are intercepted and cut off, but on the public road, every boy, every passing herd of sheep or cows gives them a lift."

From "Notes of a Walker," *Scribner's Monthly*, 1880

NAME	OCCASION	YEAR

JULY 15

He who loves an old house
Never loves in vain,
How can an old house
Used to sun and rain,
To lilac and larkspur,
And an elm above,
Ever fail to answer
The heart that gives it love?

From *Old House*
by Isabel Fiske Conant

JULY 16

JULY 17

"Make hay while the sun shines."

Miguel de Cervantes

NAME	OCCASION	YEAR

JULY 18

JULY 19

JULY 20

JULY 21

F

ill your baskets high
    With fennel green and golden pines,
Savory latter-mint and columbines,
Cool parsley, basil sweet and sunny thyme,
Yea, every flower and leaf of every clime
All gathered in the dewy morning.

From *Endymion* by John Keats

NAME	OCCASION	YEAR
JULY 22		
JULY 23		
JULY 24		

Thou wast all that to me, love,
    For which my soul did pine—
A green isle in the sea, love,
    A fountain and a shrine,
All wreathed with fairy fruits and flowers,
    And all the flowers were mine.
From *To One in Paradise* by Edgar Allan Poe

NAME	OCCASION	YEAR

JULY 25

JULY 26

JULY 27

JULY 28

HOSEA JOSÉ AND HIS HOSE

Hosea José chose a hose he needed for his lawn—
Chose the hose he knows the best is; uses it at dawn.
From the hose that Hosea chose there flows a steady stream;
'Mid the roses Hosea's hose is useful, too, I deem.

Now this hose that Hosea chose is not his hose, they say;
Though he chose the hose, he knows for it he did not pay;
Owes he for the hose he chose, and therefore, I suppose,
Where'er goes he, Hosea José knows he owes for hose.

By Arthur J. Burdick, *St. Nicholas magazine*, November 1903

NAME	OCCASION	YEAR
JULY 29		
JULY 30		
JULY 31		

~AUGUST~

August brings the sheaves of corn,
Then the harvest home is borne.

BIRTHSTONES: PERIDOT, SARDONYX   FLOWERS OF THE MONTH: GLADIOLUS, POPPY

AUGUST

NAME	OCCASION	YEAR

AUGUST 1

AUGUST 2

AUGUST 3

The lark is up to greet the sun,
 The bee is on the wing;
The ant its labor has begun,
 The woods with music ring.

From *The Sun Is Up*
by Jane Taylor

Prim little scholars are the flowers of her garden,
     Trained to stand in rows, and asking if they please.
I might love them well but for loving more the wild ones—
     O my wild ones! they tell me more than these.

From *Love in the Valley* by George Meredith

NAME	OCCASION	YEAR

AUGUST 4

AUGUST 5

AUGUST 6

AUGUST 7

A Recipe for Potpourri

For the best, most fragrant potpourri, pick well-scented flowers fresh, in the morning after the dew has dried. Remove all the petals and spread them in a thin layer over a piece of window screening or a stretched piece of cheesecloth. When the petals are dry and flexible like soft glove leather, put them on a sheet of newspaper to complete their drying. Mix the petals and add a scent fixative such as a little fruit peel or some herbs or spices. Sweet basil, mint, bay, lemon balm and marjoram are particularly good herbs for potpourri. Store the mixture in glass jars for several months, and shake the jars occasionally. The longer they remain in jars, the stronger their fragrance will become. When matured, potpourri can be used in organdy or taffeta sachets, or kept in a potpourri jar which has a special pierced lid.

NAME	OCCASION	YEAR
AUGUST 8		
AUGUST 9		
AUGUST 10		

NAME	OCCASION	YEAR

AUGUST 11

AUGUST 12

AUGUST 13

AUGUST 14

S

age is singularly good for the head and the brain; it quickeneth the senses and the memory; strengtheneth the sinews; restoreth health to those that hath the palsy; and takes away shaky trembling of the members."

John Gerard

NAME	OCCASION	YEAR
AUGUST 15		
AUGUST 16		
AUGUST 17		

NAME	OCCASION	YEAR

AUGUST 18

AUGUST 19

AUGUST 20

AUGUST 21

So we grew together,
Like to a double cherry, seeming parted,
But yet an union in partition—
Two lovely berries moulded on one stem."

From *A Midsummer-Night's Dream* by William Shakespeare

NAME	OCCASION	YEAR
	AUGUST 22	
	AUGUST 23	
	AUGUST 24	

"It's but little good you'll do watering last year's crops."

From *Adam Bede* by George Eliot

NAME	OCCASION	YEAR

AUGUST 25

AUGUST 26

AUGUST 27

AUGUST 28

NAME	OCCASION	YEAR

AUGUST 29

AUGUST 30

AUGUST 31

❧SEPTEMBER❧

September blow soft
Till the fruit's in the loft.

BIRTHSTONE: SAPPHIRE

FLOWERS OF THE MONTH: MORNING GLORY, ASTER

I send a little flower,
My messenger to be;
Let it whisper in thine ear
All I would say to thee.

Old Valentine verse

NAME	OCCASION	YEAR

SEPTEMBER 1

SEPTEMBER 2

SEPTEMBER 3

"Ne'er the rose without the thorn."

Robert Herrick

NAME	OCCASION	YEAR

SEPTEMBER 4

SEPTEMBER 5

SEPTEMBER 6

SEPTEMBER 7

ROSE VINEGAR

"Red roses, picked and dried, of them—½ pound; best vinegar, 8 pounds. Macerate for a fortnight, with occasional stirring, and strain; then filter."

From *Scammell's Treasure-House of Knowledge, 1891*
Note: this is not salad vinegar.

NAME	OCCASION	YEAR

SEPTEMBER 8

SEPTEMBER 9

SEPTEMBER 10

NAME	OCCASION	YEAR

SEPTEMBER 11

SEPTEMBER 12

SEPTEMBER 13

SEPTEMBER 14

CABBAGE PUDDING

Boil the cabbage till tender, chop fine and add four eggs, well beaten, one pound bread crumbs, one teacup melted butter, milk enough to make it as thick as mush, salt and pepper to the taste. Bake in a dish till the eggs and milk are cooked. — *Mrs. McDaniel.*"

From *Housekeeping in Old Virginia*, 1879

NAME	OCCASION	YEAR

SEPTEMBER 15

_____
_____
_____
_____
_____
_____

SEPTEMBER 16

_____
_____
_____
_____
_____

SEPTEMBER 17

_____
_____
_____
_____
_____

POISON IVY: SOME REMEDIES

Almost anything that will dissolve and remove the blistering oil of the plant, which gets on your skin when you rub against it:

- ❖ Hot water, as hot as you can stand it.
- ❖ Hot water, with a little salt in it.
- ❖ Hot soapy water.
- ❖ Hot water with baking soda in it.
- ❖ Alcohol.

NAME	OCCASION	YEAR

SEPTEMBER 18

SEPTEMBER 19

**REMEDY FOR
POISON OAK**

Make a strong
decoction of the leaves
or bark of the common willow.
Bathe the parts affected
frequently with this decoction,
and it will be found a very
efficacious remedy. —*Gen. M.*"

From *Housekeeping in Old Virginia*,
1879

SEPTEMBER 20

SEPTEMBER 21

THAT'S THE WAY!

Just a little every day,
   That's the way
Seeds in darkness swell and grow,
Tiny blades push through the snow.
Never any flower of May
Leaps to blossom in a burst.
Slowly—slowly—at the first.
   That's the way!
Just a little every day.

Just a little every day,
   That's the way!
Children learn to read and write,
Bit by bit, and mite by mite.
Never any one, I say,
Leaps to knowledge and its power.
Slowly—slowly—hour by hour.
   That's the way!
Just a little every day.

By Ella Wheeler Wilcox,
St. Nicholas magazine, June 1892

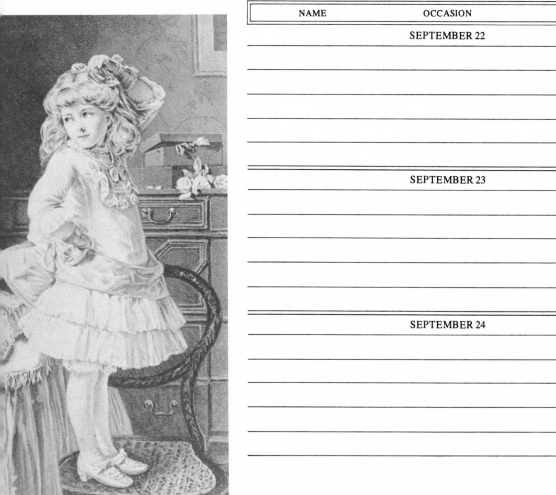

NAME	OCCASION	YEAR
SEPTEMBER 22		
SEPTEMBER 23		
SEPTEMBER 24		

NAME	OCCASION	YEAR

SEPTEMBER 25

SEPTEMBER 26

SEPTEMBER 27

SEPTEMBER 28

It was only a glad "Good morning,"
As she passed along the way,
But it spread the morning's glory
Over the livelong day.

From *Good Morning* by Charlotte Augusta Perry

NAME	OCCASION	YEAR
SEPTEMBER 29		
SEPTEMBER 30		

OCTOBER

Fresh October brings the pheasant;
Then to gather nuts is pleasant.

BIRTHSTONES: OPAL, TOURMALINE   **FLOWERS OF THE MONTH: CALENDULA, MARIGOLD**

, it sets my hart a-clickin' like the tickin' of a clock,
When the frost is on the punkin and the fodder's in the shock

From *When the Frost is on the Punkin* by James Whitcomb Riley

NAME	OCCASION	YEAR

OCTOBER 1

OCTOBER 2

OCTOBER 3

NAME	OCCASION	YEAR

OCTOBER 4

OCTOBER 5

OCTOBER 6

OCTOBER 7

. . . I sally forth, half sad, half proud,
And I come to the velvet, imperial crowd,
The wine-red, the gold, the crimson, the pied, —
The dahlias that reign by the garden-side.
From *Frost Tonight* by Edith M. Thomas

NAME	OCCASION	YEAR

OCTOBER 8

OCTOBER 9

OCTOBER 10

Heaven from all creatures hides the book of Fate,
All but the page prescrib'd, their present state.

From *Essay on Man*, by Alexander Pope

NAME	OCCASION	YEAR

OCTOBER 11

OCTOBER 12

OCTOBER 13

OCTOBER 14

"Dried tops of large and small wormwood, rosemary, sage, mint, rue, lavender flowers, of each 2 ounces; calamus root, cinnamon, cloves, nutmeg, garlic, of each ½ ounce. Camphor, ½ ounce. Concentrated acetic acid, 2 ounces. Strong vinegar, 8 pounds. Macerate the herbs and spices in the vinegar for a fortnight; strain, press and add the camphor dissolved in the acetic acid."

Note: this is not salad vinegar, but an aromatic vinegar as described the week of January 15.

From *Scammell's Treasure-House of Knowledge 1891*

NAME	OCCASION	YEAR
OCTOBER 15		
OCTOBER 16		
OCTOBER 17		

"You cannot forget if you would, those golden kisses all over the cheeks of the meadow, queerly called dandelions."

From *Star Papers* by Henry Ward Beecher

NAME	OCCASION	YEAR

OCTOBER 18

OCTOBER 19

OCTOBER 20

OCTOBER 21

October gave a party;
The leaves by hundreds came:

NAME	OCCASION	YEAR
OCTOBER 22		
OCTOBER 23		
OCTOBER 24		

The ashes, oaks, and maples,
   And those of every name.

From *October's Party* by George Cooper

NAME	OCCASION	YEAR

OCTOBER 25

OCTOBER 26

OCTOBER 27

OCTOBER 28

These are the days when birds
come back,
A very few, a bird or two,
To take a backward look.

From *First Series. Nature, XXVII, Indian Summer*,
by Emily Dickinson

NAME	OCCASION	YEAR

OCTOBER 29

OCTOBER 30

OCTOBER 31

NOVEMBER

Dull November brings the blast;
Then the leaves are whirling fast.

BIRTHSTONE: TOPAZ   FLOWER OF THE MONTH: CHRYSANTHEMUM

Henceforth I shall know
That Nature ne'er deserts the wise and pure;
No plot so narrow, be but Nature there,
No waste so vacant, but may well employ
Each faculty of sense, and keep the heart
Awake to Love and Beauty!

Samuel Taylor Coleridge

NAME	OCCASION	YEAR

NOVEMBER 1

NOVEMBER 2

NOVEMBER 3

I heard a thousand blended notes,
While in a grove I sate reclined,
In that sweet mood when pleasant thoughts
Bring sad thoughts to the mind.

From *Lines Written in Early Spring*
by William Wordsworth

NAME	OCCASION	YEAR

NOVEMBER 4

NOVEMBER 5

NOVEMBER 6

NOVEMBER 7

FIRST SNOW

The cows are bawling in the mountains.
The snowflakes fall.
They are leaving the pools and pebbled fountains;
Troubled, they bawl.
They are winding down the mountain's shoulders
Through the open pines,
Through wild rose thickets and the granite bowlders
In broken lines.
Each calf trots close beside its mother
And so they go,
Bawling and calling to one another
About the snow.

Charles E. S. Wood

NAME	OCCASION	YEAR

NOVEMBER 8

NOVEMBER 9

NOVEMBER 10

"The ornament of a house is the friends who frequent it."

From *Society and Solitude*, *Domestic Life* by Ralph Waldo Emerson

NAME	OCCASION	YEAR

NOVEMBER 11

NOVEMBER 12

NOVEMBER 13

NOVEMBER 14

Evil Weevils

In granaries corn is subject to be destroyed by the weevil, moth, and beetle: frequent screening, stirring, and exposing to draught of wind or fresh air, will prevent these insects injuring it, and will destroy their eggs if laid among it. Should this have been neglected, and the insects appear in the winged state, a hen or hens with new hatched chickens, will free it entirely of the insects without feeding, or very sparingly, on the corn.

"It is said that the leaves of pellitory of the wall (an herb so called from growing on walls) will destroy the weevil in corn; and that the smell of lobsters also proves fatal to them."

From *The Pennsylvania Farmer*
by Job Roberts, 1804

NAME	OCCASION	YEAR
NOVEMBER 15		
NOVEMBER 16		
NOVEMBER 17		

NAME	OCCASION	YEAR

NOVEMBER 18

NOVEMBER 19

NOVEMBER 20

NOVEMBER 21

hen here's to the oak, the brave old oak,
   Who stands in his pride alone!
And still flourish he, a hale green tree,
   When a hundred years are gone!

From *The Brave Old Oak* by Henry Fothergill Chorley

NAME	OCCASION	YEAR
NOVEMBER 22		
NOVEMBER 23		
NOVEMBER 24		

NAME	OCCASION	YEAR

NOVEMBER 25

NOVEMBER 26

NOVEMBER 27

NOVEMBER 28

NAME	OCCASION	YEAR
NOVEMBER 29		

NOVEMBER 30

An old-fashioned remedy for rheumatism was to put three potatoes in your pockets and carry them about!

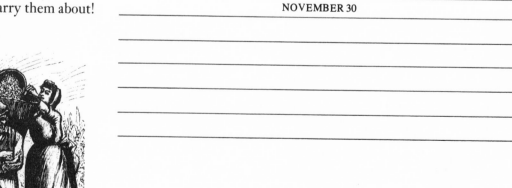

DECEMBER

Chill December brings the sleet,
Blazing fire, and Christmas treat.

BIRTHSTONES: TURQUOISE, ZIRCON   FLOWERS OF THE MONTH: HOLLY, NARCISSUS, POINSETTIA

"Canary-birds feed on sugar and seed,
Parrots have crackers to crunch;
And as for the poodles, they tell me the noodles
Have chickens and cream for their lunch.
But there's never a question
About MY digestion—
ANYTHING does for me!"
From *The Plaint of the Camel* by Charles Edward Carryl

NAME	OCCASION	YEAR

DECEMBER 1

DECEMBER 2

DECEMBER 3

"When the bread rises in the oven, the heart of the housewife rises with it."

Frederika Bremer

NAME	OCCASION	YEAR

DECEMBER 4

DECEMBER 5

DECEMBER 6

DECEMBER 7

Love is like the wild rose-briar;
   Friendship like the holly-tree.
The holly is dark when the rose-briar blooms,
   But which will bloom most constantly?

From *Love and Friendship* by Emily Brontë

NAME	OCCASION	YEAR

DECEMBER 8

DECEMBER 9

DECEMBER 10

"The proof of the pudding is in the eating."

Miguel de Cervantes

NAME	OCCASION	YEAR

DECEMBER 11

DECEMBER 12

DECEMBER 13

DECEMBER 14

NAME	OCCASION	YEAR

DECEMBER 15

DECEMBER 16

DECEMBER 17

A pine tree stands so lonely
  In the North where the high winds blow,
He sleeps; and the whitest blanket
  Wraps him in ice and snow.

Heinrich Heine

NAME	OCCASION	YEAR

DECEMBER 18

DECEMBER 19

DECEMBER 20

DECEMBER 21

GREETINGS FROM THE SOUTH.

NAME	OCCASION	YEAR

DECEMBER 22

DECEMBER 23

DECEMBER 24

"The only gift is a portion of thyself."

Ralph Waldo Emerson

NAME	OCCASION	YEAR

DECEMBER 25

_____

_____

_____

_____

_____

_____

DECEMBER 26

_____

_____

_____

_____

I think I could turn and live with
    animals, they are so placid
    and self-contain'd.

From *Song of Myself* by Walt Whitman

DECEMBER 27

_____

_____

_____

_____

_____

DECEMBER 28

_____

_____

_____

_____

_____

HOUSE BLESSING

Stand firm, gray Rock!
    Tough-weathered Beams,
        hold fast!
Stanch Walls, proud Roof,
    Repel the warring Blast!
Glow warm, deep Hearth,
    Against the Winter's Chill;
Clear Flame of Love,
    Burn brighter, warmer still!
    Arthur Guiterman

NAME	OCCASION	YEAR

DECEMBER 29

DECEMBER 30

DECEMBER 31

SIGNS OF THE ZODIAC

The Ram, the Bull, and the Heavenly Twins,
And next the Crab, the Lion shines,
The Virgin and the Scales,
The Scorpion, Archer, and He-Goat,
The Man that carries the Watering-pot,
The Fish with the glittering tails.

Aries
March 21 to April 19

Taurus
April 20 to May 20

Gemini
May 21 to June 20

Cancer
June 21 to July 22

Leo
July 23 to August 22

Virgo
August 23 to September 22

Libra
September 23 to October 22

Scorpio
October 23 to November 21

Sagittarius
November 22 to December 21

Capricorn
December 22 to January 19

Aquarius
January 20 to February 18

Pisces
February 19 to March 20

WEDDING ANNIVERSARY GIFTS

It has long been the custom to give anniversary gifts. All the anniversaries up to the fifteenth now have special gifts, and every fifth one after that is also commemorated. Successive gifts are made of materials ever increasing in intrinsic value. They have not always been in exactly the same order (for example, at the turn-of-the-century the first was the cotton anniversary, the second the paper), nor have there been until fairly recently so many choices for a particular anniversary. The list that follows is a combination of the old and the new, and the traditional gifts from late Victorian times are italicized.

1st	*Paper*, plastic
2nd	*Cotton*
3rd	*Leather*, leatherlike material
4th	Silk, linen, rayon, nylon, synthetic silks
5th	Wood, decorative accessories for home
6th	Iron
7th	*Wool*, copper, brass
8th	Bronze, electric appliances
9th	Pottery, china, glass
10th	*Tin*, aluminum
11th	Steel
12th	*Linen, silk*
13th	Lace
14th	Ivory, agate
15th	*Crystal*, glass
20th	*China*, porcelain
25th	*Silver*
30th	*Pearl*, personal gifts
35th	Coral, jade
40th	*Ruby*, garnet
45th	Sapphire, tourmaline
50th	*Gold*
55th	Emerald, turquoise
60th	Diamond
75th	*Diamond*, gold

GIFTS WITH SPECIAL MEANING

It is sometimes difficult, when the time is hard upon you, to think of a gift which would have personal meaning for a friend or family member. Use the spaces here to take notes and remind yourself of the favorite things—be they hummingbirds or dahlias, Wordsworth or Mother Goose, burnt orange or royal purple—of people to whom you wish to give something special.

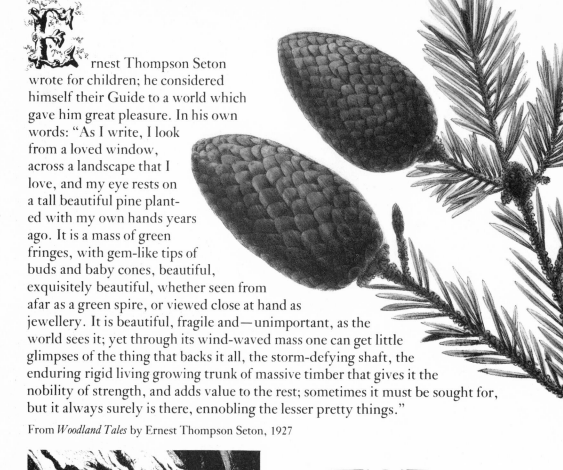

Ernest Thompson Seton wrote for children; he considered himself their Guide to a world which gave him great pleasure. In his own words: "As I write, I look from a loved window, across a landscape that I love, and my eye rests on a tall beautiful pine plant-ed with my own hands years ago. It is a mass of green fringes, with gem-like tips of buds and baby cones, beautiful, exquisitely beautiful, whether seen from afar as a green spire, or viewed close at hand as jewellery. It is beautiful, fragile and—unimportant, as the world sees it; yet through its wind-waved mass one can get little glimpses of the thing that backs it all, the storm-defying shaft, the enduring rigid living growing trunk of massive timber that gives it the nobility of strength, and adds value to the rest; sometimes it must be sought for, but it always surely is there, ennobling the lesser pretty things."

From *Woodland Tales* by Ernest Thompson Seton, 1927

THE WOODCRAFT KALENDAR

Snow Moon	*January*
Hunger Moon	*February*
Wakening Moon	*March*
Grass Moon	*April*
Planting Moon	*May*
Rose Moon	*June*
Thunder Moon	*July*
Red Moon	*August*
Hunting Moon	*September*
Falling-Leaf Moon	*October*
Mad Moon	*November*
Long-Night Moon	*December*

From *Woodland Tales*
by Ernest Thompson Seton, 1927